Original title:
Whispers of Divine Grace

Copyright © 2024 Book Fairy Publishing
All rights reserved.

Author: Elias Seraphim
ISBN HARDBACK: 978-9916-87-855-2
ISBN PAPERBACK: 978-9916-87-856-9

## Murmurs of the Sacred Heart

In silence, whispers soft and light,
The sacred heart glows through the night.
With every pulse, a loving grace,
Calls us to seek a holy place.

Through trials faced and shadows cast,
The heart's sweet murmur shall hold fast.
A promise made, forever true,
In every breath, it beckons you.

## Radiance of Unfailing Hope

From dawn's first light to twilight's end,
The radiance shines, a faithful friend.
In valleys deep, it guides the way,
Bringing warmth to the coldest day.

Each glimmer speaks of love divine,
A promise sealed by sacred sign.
In despair's clutch, let your heart cope,
For in the dark, there blooms the hope.

## **Graceful Shadows of the Divine**

In the twilight where shadows dance,
The divine whispers, offering chance.
Grace unfolds in each soft sigh,
As souls connect beyond the sky.

When burdens weigh and hearts grow weak,
In shadows' grace, the spirit speaks.
Through every trial, we shall find,
The gentle touch of love aligned.

## The Gentle Call of the Spirit

A still, small voice within the night,
Calls forth the soul to seek the light.
In quiet moments, hearts will yield,
To the spirit's soft, comforting shield.

Through storms of life, when doubts arise,
The spirit's call will never die.
Embrace the peace, let burdens cease,
In every whisper, find your peace.

## The Celestial Canvas of Hope

Stars weave tales in the night sky,
Dreams await on the winds up high.
Each twinkle whispers a promise near,
Guiding the hearts that hold love dear.

Colors blend in the dawn's embrace,
A canvas bright, each stroke a grace.
From shadows deep, light breaks anew,
Painting the world with a vibrant hue.

## Gentle Caresses from Eden's Hand

The breeze carries whispers of love,
Soft touches sent from above.
Nature sings in every bloom,
A fragrance sweet, dispelling gloom.

Rivers flow with a soothing song,
Reminding us where we belong.
In sacred woods where spirits dwell,
Each leaf tells stories we know well.

## The Stillness of Knowing

In silence deep, the truth unfolds,
Whispers of wisdom, ancient gold.
The heart beats steady, wrapped in calm,
A sacred peace, a healing balm.

Moments linger, timeless and pure,
In stillness, our souls find a cure.
Each breath we take, a prayer in grace,
The universe cradles us in embrace.

## Dances in the Meadow of Belief

In fields of green, the spirit leaps,
The dance of faith, a joy that keeps.
Every step, a rhythm divine,
Unity in all, the sacred sign.

Sunlight glimmers on blades of grass,
Illuminating paths we dare to pass.
With each twirl, hearts are set free,
A heavenly chorus in harmony.

## Secrets of Joy in the Morning Light

In the dawn's embrace, whispers arise,
Softly speaking of love in the skies.
Each ray of sun, a promise anew,
Echoes of grace, in the morning dew.

Heaven's song weaves through the air,
Filling hearts with a beauty rare.
Joy blooms bright in light's gentle kiss,
A sacred moment, a taste of bliss.

Birds sing praises, the world comes alive,
In the dance of dawn, spirits thrive.
With every breath, the soul takes flight,
Finding secrets in the morning light.

All worries fade with the sun's rise,
In gratitude, we lift our eyes.
For in this wonder, joy takes its place,
A testament to love's sweet grace.

## The Eternal Dance of Affection and Grace

In the stillness, hearts intertwine,
A sacred rhythm, a love divine.
With every beat, our spirits converge,
In the dance of life, we find the urge.

Grace flows softly like a winding stream,
In the melody of a shared dream.
Together we twirl in the light of faith,
Embracing the bonds we choose to create.

Time whispers secrets in shadows cast,
While love's gentle touch holds our hearts fast.
In every moment, our souls take flight,
Bathed in the glow of eternal light.

With open arms, we journey as one,
Through trials and joys, until the day is done.
For in this dance, we find our place,
In the eternal embrace of affection and grace.

# The Veil of Quiet Grace

Beneath the silent folds of night,
A gentle whisper calls the soul,
In stillness, we embrace the light,
Where hearts and heavens become whole.

Each breath, a prayer upon the breeze,
Each thought, a journey towards the divine,
In sacred stillness, spirits seize,
The quiet grace that makes us shine.

The veil is thin, the day does fade,
In twilight's glow, we find our peace,
In truths unsaid, in love conveyed,
Our hearts rejoice, our fears release.

Together we walk, hand in hand,
Through whispered paths of faith and love,
In every grain of golden sand,
We find the touch of God above.

## Sunlight on the Spirit's Journey

With dawn's embrace, the shadows flee,
As sunlight spills on open fields,
It warms the soul, sets spirits free,
The heart to hope and joy it wields.

Each step we take, a dance in grace,
The path illuminated bright,
We seek the truth in every place,
As spirits soar towards the light.

In every heartbeat, faith ignites,
A promise sung in morning's glow,
In struggles faced, in love that fights,
We find the strength that helps us grow.

The journey winds like rivers flow,
Through valleys deep and mountains high,
In praise we rise, as soft winds blow,
To touch the endless, azure sky.

## Anointed Paths of Quietude

Along the way where silence sighs,
The gentle footsteps mark the earth,
In shadows cast, our spirit tries,
To seek the promise of rebirth.

Anointed paths, where waters flow,
In tranquil shades of evening's balm,
The heart learns well, for it will know,
The peace that comes, a healing calm.

Beneath the trees, in soft repose,
We find the wisdom that endures,
In every petal's quiet pose,
A glimpse of grace that nature cures.

Together we wander, lost yet found,
In sacred rhythms of the night,
With every step, the holy ground,
Awaits the dawn, the purest light.

## **Celestial Murmurings Beneath the Stars**

Beneath the canopy of dreams,
The stars alight on velvet skies,
In softest whispers, the cosmos gleams,
Each twinkle shared, a love that ties.

In night's embrace, our spirits soar,
We feel the world's celestial grace,
As constellations gently pour,
Their ancient tales in time and space.

The moon, our guide, in silvered hue,
Bestows a glow on weary hearts,
With every glance, the night feels new,
A spark ignites, and fears depart.

With stars as witnesses, we tread,
The paths where light and shadows play,
In unity, our prayers are spread,
Celestial murmurings lead the way.

## Love Letters from the Heavens

In silence, whispers fill the air,
Messages sent with tender care.
Each star a note, each moon a sigh,
From realms above where angels fly.

Softly they brush against our hearts,
With every beat, love never departs.
Boundless grace in the darkest night,
Guiding our souls with radiant light.

## **Embracing the Eternal Promise**

In every heartbeat lies a vow,
A sacred promise made right now.
Beyond the veil of time and space,
Love endures, filled with divine grace.

Through trials faced and joys bestowed,
The path of faith is brightly showed.
Eternity whispers, 'You are mine,'
In every moment, love's design.

## **Divine Comfort in Human Struggles**

In shadows cast by burdens deep,
The light of grace will softly creep.
In trials faced, we find His hand,
A gentle touch on shifting sand.

With whispered words through darkest night,
He guides our hearts to seek the light.
When tears like rivers start to flow,
His love will cradle, heal, and grow.

## The Kindness Beneath Each Moment

In every breath, a spark divine,
In every touch, His love will shine.
Amidst the rush, we often miss,
The quiet grace in every kiss.

With open hearts and hands to lend,
We share the love that knows no end.
In fleeting time, the truth remains,
Kindness blooms through joys and pains.

## The Promise of Dawn Beyond the Valley

When shadows stretch and hope seems lost,
A dawn will rise, no matter the cost.
The valley low may seem so wide,
But in His arms, we safely abide.

With each new day, the light will break,
Reviving hearts, our spirits wake.
The promise sworn, a gift so dear,
For every prayer, He draws us near.

## The Silent Vigil of Heartfelt Prayers

In quiet moments, souls align,
With whispered hopes, our hearts entwine.
The silence speaks of love profound,
In steadfast faith, we're safe and sound.

As candles flicker in the dark,
Each prayer ignites a sacred spark.
In solitude, we find our way,
Through heartfelt prayers, we humbly sway.

## **A Pilgrimage of Heart and Soul**

In the quiet of the morning light,
We wander paths of dreams and grace,
Each step a prayer, a whispered plight,
Seeking solace in this sacred space.

With every breath, a burden shed,
Our hearts entwined in love so pure,
The whispers of the faithful dead,
Guide our way, their spirits sure.

Together we traverse the hills,
Through valleys dark, we courage find,
Each challenge faced, the spirit thrills,
With every trial, our souls aligned.

As pilgrims sworn to seek the light,
We journey on, hand in hand,
Embracing both the day and night,
In this, our faith, forever stand.

**Streams of Grace Flowing Evergreen**

In the forest deep, where shadows dwell,
The waters sing a hymn divine,
With gentle ripples, secrets tell,
Of love that flows through roots and vine.

Through leaves that dance in breezes light,
The whispers of the ancients call,
Life flourishes under heaven's sight,
In every rise, in every fall.

The streams of grace, they glisten bright,
Invoking peace in hearts once torn,
A touch of hope, a guiding light,
From morning's kiss to evening's morn.

And as we drink from waters fair,
Our spirits bloom, in faith we grow,
United in this sacred prayer,
In streams of grace, our souls shall flow.

**Tides of Mercy at the Dawn's Break**

As dawn unfolds its golden hue,
The tides of mercy rise and fall,
With every wave, a heart made new,
A gentle, loving, sacred call.

With each soft blush the sky unfolds,
The world awakens, hope reborn,
A promise hidden, grace foretold,
In every breath, the light is sworn.

Through trials faced and battles fought,
The ocean's heartbeat guides our way,
In mercy's flow, our burdens caught,
A tranquil balm for each new day.

Together, we embrace the morn,
With faith ablaze, our spirits soar,
In tides of mercy, love is sworn,
Forever bound, forevermore.

## Faith in the Flicker of a Candle

In the stillness of the night,
A candle's glow, a steady flame,
It flickers softly, pure and bright,
A beacon whispering Your name.

With every shadow that it casts,
A story of hope and love unfolds,
A promise held through storms that pass,
In faith, our hearts, like candles, hold.

Through trials dark and doubts that creep,
The flicker stands, a steadfast guide,
In silence sweet, our spirits leap,
For in that light, our hopes abide.

So let us cherish this gentle light,
Together, with our hearts aglow,
In faith's embrace, we find our might,
With every flicker, love will grow.

## **Glimmers of Transcendent Love**

In the silence of the night, we find,
A love that stretches beyond time.
Stars whisper secrets to the heart,
Binding souls that shall not part.

Faith like a river softly flows,
Washing over doubts that only grow.
In every glimmer, hope resides,
A sacred light where love abides.

Among the shadows, courage shines,
Guided by whispers of divine signs.
Every moment, a precious gift,
In transcendent love, our spirits lift.

Together, we stand hand in hand,
In the warmth of a promised land.
Glimmers of love, forever bright,
Lead us through the darkest night.

## **Breath of the Infinite**

Inhale the grace of dawn's embrace,
Each breath a prayer, a sacred space.
Exhale the fears that cloud the mind,
In the breath of the infinite, peace we find.

With every heartbeat, a hymn is sung,
To the One who beckons, old and young.
Life's tapestry with threads of gold,
A story of mercy, tenderly told.

Mountains rise to meet the skies,
In nature's wonder, the soul complies.
Breath flows freely, a divine art,
Connecting the heavens to every heart.

In the stillness, hear the call,
The infinite whispers, love encompasses all.
In the dance of existence, we unite,
As breath of the infinite fuels our light.

## **Caresses from Above**

Softly, like a feather's touch,
Grace descends, embracing much.
In the morning's light we see,
Caresses from Above, setting us free.

In laughter shared, or tears that flow,
Divine presence, we come to know.
With gentle nudges, hearts are stirred,
Each moment cherished, love's sweet word.

Through trials faced, we find our way,
By the guidance of light each day.
Caresses of hope in times of fear,
Whispers of comfort, always near.

In the vastness of stars above,
We find solace, wrapped in love.
Each caress a blessing from the skies,
Filling our spirits, teaching us to rise.

## **Lullabies of the Celestial Choir**

Underneath the moon's soft glow,
Angels sing, their voices flow.
Lullabies drift on the night air,
Whispers of love, banishing despair.

Cradled in the arms of dreams,
In sacred realms, the heart redeems.
Every note a precious thread,
Binding the living to the dead.

With each refrain, the soul takes flight,
Lost in melodies of purest light.
United in harmony's embrace,
Lullabies weave a sacred space.

As the universe hums along,
We sway together, a timeless song.
In the hush of night, we find our way,
With lullabies that never stray.

## Faint Echoes in the Chamber of the Heart

In the stillness, whispers grow,
Faint echoes of love, they flow.
Hearts entwined in sacred grace,
Finding solace in this space.

Soft prayers rise on gentle wings,
A melody of hope it brings.
In shadows deep, the light breaks through,
Guiding us to what is true.

Through trials faced, our spirits soar,
Bound by faith, forevermore.
Each heartbeat sings a sacred hymn,
In the quiet, love won't dim.

In chambers deep where shadows dwell,
Divine presence casts a spell.
With every breath, we draw it near,
Faint echoes whisper, pure and clear.

**Moonlit Reflections of Divine Favor**

Underneath the silver glow,
Moonlit tides of grace do flow.
Guiding hearts through night's embrace,
Reflecting love in every trace.

Stars align in heavens wide,
With each twinkle, dreams abide.
The night reveals a holy sign,
In shadows, we feel the divine.

In tranquil pools, the light does dance,
A sacred moment, a second chance.
We rise and fall, like ebbing tide,
In moonlit grace, our fears subside.

With every beam, a truth is born,
From darkest night, a new dawn's sworn.
In reflections, our souls aspire,
Finding peace in the holy fire.

## **A Symphony of Souls in Harmony**

In the quiet, hearts unite,
A symphony of love takes flight.
Voices blend in sacred song,
Together, we are ever strong.

Each note rises, pure and clear,
Resonating far and near.
With every chord, a spirit free,
In harmony, our destiny.

Through valleys deep and mountains tall,
We stand together, we won't fall.
A dance of joy, a shared refrain,
In collective heart, we break the chain.

In every beat, a story told,
Of faith unyielding and love bold.
As souls entwine in holy peace,
This symphony shall never cease.

## Kindled Flames of Spiritual Awakening

In the darkness, fires bloom,
Kindled flames dispel the gloom.
Hearts ignited, spirits rise,
Awakening beneath the skies.

Through the ashes, light breaks free,
A dance of souls in unity.
With every spark, a truth ignites,
Illuminating sacred nights.

In fervent glow, we find our way,
Guided by the light of day.
These flames of faith, a guiding star,
Leading us ever near and far.

As embers glow, we gather close,
In the warmth, the heart's repose.
Kindled flames shall lead us home,
In awakened souls, love's sweet roam.

## The Compassionate Touch of the Divine

In stillness, the heart finds grace,
A whisper of love in the quiet space.
Guided hands, gentle and kind,
Reminding us of the truth we seek to find.

Through trials and sorrows, We journey along,
A balm for the weary, the weary are strong.
With faith as our anchor, we rise and we soar,
Together in spirit, forever we adore.

The light of compassion, a beacon to share,
Hearts intertwined in the warmest prayer.
From depths of despair, we gather and weave,
Threads of forgiveness, in which we believe.

Oh, sacred embrace, hold us so tight,
In the soft glow of love, we bask in the light.
Each tear that we shed, a testament true,
To the infinite mercy that's waiting for you.

**Songs of Peace from the Celestial Realms**

Listen closely, the choir sings,
A melody carried on angel's wings.
Notes of tranquility weave through the air,
A symphony born from a loving prayer.

In the quiet of night, peace gently speaks,
Comfort for the weary, treasure for the meek.
In every heart, a seed of light blooms,
Echoing harmony that dispels all glooms.

Beneath the vast heavens, stars softly glow,
Reminders of hope in the world below.
From the sigh of the wind to the wave of the sea,
Nature resounds with the song of the free.

Join the chorus, let your spirit arise,
In the depth of your being, let love be your prize.
Together we'll dance to the song that is near,
From the celestial realms, let your heart learn to hear.

## **Timeless Devotion in Endless Paths**

In the silence, a whisper calls,
To tread the paths where the spirit enthralls.
With each step, a promise, a vow,
To seek truth and love in the here and now.

The journey unfolds, an eternal embrace,
With faith as our guide through time and space.
In every moment, a chance to reflect,
On the lessons of life, we humbly collect.

Hands lifted high in prayer and praise,
Grateful hearts shine through all of the days.
Boundless devotion, a flame ever bright,
Illuminating the shadows, bringing forth light.

Together we walk, through valleys and hills,
In the depths of our beings, a peace that fulfills.
For love knows no limits, no distance, no time,
In this sacred path, our spirits will climb.

## **Benevolence Stirring in the Heart**

In every heart, a seed takes root,
Nurtured by kindness, blooming in truth.
Compassion's touch, soft as the dew,
Awakens the spirit, making all things new.

Gentle hands reaching across the divide,
In unity's presence, we stand side by side.
With open arms and courage to share,
We carry the message of love everywhere.

Moments of grace, like petals unfold,
Whispers of hope in stories retold.
A tapestry woven from kindness and care,
Shining bright, a light we all can wear.

Let love be the song that guides us each day,
A melody sweet in each word that we say.
With benevolence stirring, we rise and we start,
To transform the world from the depths of the heart.

## **The Canvas of Grace Painted in Silence**

In quiet chambers, hearts do seek,
The brush of love, gentle and meek.
Each stroke a prayer, each hue a sigh,
In silence, faith learns to fly.

Colors of hope upon the soul,
In whispers soft, they make us whole.
The canvas stretches, wide and grand,
As hands of mercy guide the hand.

Light pours in, through every seam,
Awakening dreams, like morning's gleam.
The palette rich, with shades divine,
In silent grace, our spirits align.

A masterpiece forged in the night,
With every heartbeat, we feel the light.
In silence, the artist paints anew,
A vision of love, forever true.

## **Echoes of Promise in the Twilight**

As daylight fades into the dusk,
The promises linger, sweet and brusque.
Every shadow, a whisper's call,
In twilight's glow, we rise, we fall.

A symphony sung in colors bold,
Of ancient vows, and stories told.
In the echo, we find our place,
Within the arms of boundless grace.

Stars emerge in a velvet sky,
As hope ignites, let worries die.
In lingering light, our spirits soar,
For every ending births a door.

The night unveils the dreams we chase,
With every heartbeat, we embrace.
In echoes soft, the dawn awaits,
A promise kept, as love creates.

## **Celestial Murmurs of Renewal**

In the stillness, stars do hum,
Songs of old, in whispers come.
Each note a sign, a light aglow,
Of life reborn, where rivers flow.

The cosmos speaks in tender ways,
With gentle hints of brighter days.
As darkness yields to morning light,
Our hearts awaken to the sight.

Clouds drift softly, dreams take flight,
In the embrace of holy night.
The murmurs weave a tapestry,
Of grace and love, eternally.

In every flicker, we are found,
In sacred hush, redemption's sound.
Together under cosmic beams,
We find our hope within our dreams.

## The Unfolding Petals of Spiritual Blossoms

In gardens rich, the blossoms bloom,
Petals unfold, dispelling gloom.
With every dawn, a fresh embrace,
Each flower speaks of boundless grace.

The fragrance wafts, in spirit's air,
Inviting hearts to pause and share.
In colors bright, the truth reveals,
The sacred bond that love conceals.

Nature's hymn, a soft refrain,
Of sacred joy and sweet refrain.
In blooms that flourish, we discover,
The divine touch of one another.

As petals fall, new life will rise,
In cycles grand, beneath the skies.
Embrace the blooms, let spirits blend,
For in each blossom, love transcends.

## The Unseen Glow of Unfailing Love

In shadows deep, Your light will roam,
A beacon bright, a guiding home.
In silence heard, Your whispers call,
Embracing hearts, uplifting all.

Through trials faced, Your hand we'll find,
In every tear, Your love unbinds.
With steadfast grace, You pave the way,
A constant flame, both night and day.

From weary paths, we seek the shore,
Your mercy flows, forevermore.
In every glance, we see the truth,
The unseen glow of love's sweet youth.

With every breath, we sing Your praise,
In sacred moments, hearts ablaze.
United souls in reverent prayer,
In Your embrace, we find our share.

## **A Dialogue with the Infinite**

In stillness sought, the heart will yearn,
For whispers soft, from fires that burn.
A sacred bond in silence found,
In questions posed on holy ground.

Oh Infinite, Your wisdom flows,
Your breath in winds, a gentle prose.
Each star a note in cosmic song,
In unity, we all belong.

Through trials faced, we seek the light,
In every shadow, You're the sight.
The universe, a canvas grand,
In this dialogue, we understand.

With hearts aligned, we hear the call,
In every rise, we learn to fall.
In silent awe, we journey deep,
Finding grace, the soul will keep.

## Sacred Rivers Flowing through the Soul

In gentle streams, the waters flow,
Through valleys deep, their essence glow.
Each drop a blessing, pure and free,
A sacred river flowing me.

The current swift, yet soft the grace,
In every tide, a warm embrace.
With every wave, a story told,
Of love eternal, brave and bold.

From mountains high to fields below,
The sacred rivers teach us flow.
In ebb and rise, we find our peace,
As all our fears begin to cease.

With hearts alive, we drink the sky,
In unity, the soul will fly.
In sacred whispers, learn to whole,
For love's sweet current fills the soul.

## Murmurs of the Heart's Reverie

In quiet moments, whispers speak,
The heart's soft song, a truth we seek.
With every breath, a prayer we weave,
In sacred trust, we shall believe.

In twilight dreams, the soul takes flight,
In shimmering shadows, finds the light.
With loving kindness, we embrace,
The murmurs of the heart's sweet grace.

In every glance, a story shared,
In thoughts unspoken, love is bared.
With gentle touch, we heal the pain,
In tender moments, joy we gain.

Through time's embrace, hearts intertwine,
In love's soft glow, forever shine.
With reverie, we dance and sing,
In harmony, our spirits cling.

# **Revelations in Quiet Moments**

In the stillness of dawn's embrace,
Whispers of grace fill the air.
Hearts attune to a holy space,
Finding comfort in silent prayer.

Leaves rustle with sacred song,
Nature's chorus, pure and bright.
In these moments, we all belong,
Guided softly by gentle light.

The world fades, as we reflect,
On truth revealed in soft silence.
In solitude, our faith connects,
Shining through with divine guidance.

Each breath a note in life's hymn,
A symphony of love and hope.
In quietude, spirits brim,
As we learn to heal and cope.

## **Benevolent Hands of Providence**

In the fabric of daily life,
We find threads of silver grace.
Hands that guide through toil and strife,
Holding us in a warm embrace.

Mountains rise, yet hearts soar high,
With faith as our steadfast guide.
In blessings shared, we testify,
To the love that will abide.

When shadows loom and doubts align,
We seek shelter beneath His wing.
In every trial, light will shine,
And peace will bloom, new life to bring.

Let gratitude fill our days,
For providence in joys and pain.
With open hearts, our voices raise,
To honor love where we remain.

## **Dances of Angelic Presence**

In twilight's glow, they softly glide,
Whispers of hope in every turn.
Angels gather, by our side,
Their gentle presence, hearts discern.

Through trials faced and tears they've shed,
They weave courage in the dark.
With every prayer that's daily said,
They stir the flame, igniting spark.

In laughter shared, their joy ignites,
A dance of love, pure and divine.
We feel their warmth through starry nights,
In every heartbeat, every sign.

So let us trust when life is hard,
That we are held by unseen hands.
In faith we dance, let down our guard,
For hope and peace in their commands.

## Reflections on Sacred Waters

By the river, waters flow,
Mirrors of light in sun's embrace.
Every ripple tells us so,
Of deeper truths, of sacred grace.

Beneath the surface, life abounds,
A testament to resilience bright.
In quiet depths, wisdom resounds,
Inviting hearts to seek the light.

Each drop a prayer, a story spun,
In currents strong, find peace and calm.
As the day fades, the journey's won,
Reflections soothe, a gentle balm.

In sacred waters, spirits meet,
Flowing freely, unconfined.
As one, we gather, pure and sweet,
The love of God forever binds.

## Threads of Light in the Weaving of Time

In the loom of dawn, threads unite,
Each golden strand, a glimpse of light.
Moments stitched with love divine,
Eternity dances in the sacred line.

Through shadows cast, the weaver's hand,
Crafts the stories of this land.
Wisdom flows from the ancient seam,
Guiding hearts in the woven dream.

Each breath a stitch in the fabric grand,
Every heartbeat, a sacred strand.
In the tapestry of faith, we find,
The threads of light that bind humankind.

As the stars align in the night sky's dome,
We discover in each, a piece of home.
For in this weaving, we rise and strive,
Threads of time that keep hope alive.

## Sacred Whispers on the Wind

In the hush of twilight, voices stir,
Soft as petals that gently concur.
Sacred whispers float on the breeze,
Carrying prayers from ancient trees.

Every sigh of wind, a call to pause,
Echoes of faith, in nature's laws.
Listen closely, hear the song,
Of life and love where we all belong.

Mountains bow down to the secrets they keep,
While rivers, in reverence, quietly weep.
The world spins softly on its axis,
In divine connection, we find our praxis.

So let your spirit dance with delight,
In sacred whispers, find your light.
For in the wind's gentle embrace,
We discover the heart of grace.

## Illuminations in Sacred Spaces

In the chapel's glow, candles burn bright,
Casting shadows that weave through the night.
Every flicker, a prayer sent high,
Illuminations that never die.

Amidst the silence, echoes of grace,
Hearts uplifted in this hallowed place.
Walls adorned with the stories of years,
In this sanctuary, our hope appears.

Beneath the altar, a promise lies,
In every tear, in every rise.
The soul finds solace, the spirit sings,
In sacred spaces, love's true offering.

As light streams through the stained glass panes,
We gather strength from love's refrains.
In the essence of faith, we embrace,
The illuminations in sacred space.

## The Soft Serenade of Creation


In the cradle of dawn, a melody plays,
Birds in chorus weave the day's praise.
Nature hums a gentle tune,
A soft serenade beneath the moon.

Mountains rise with a stately grace,
In every valley, a hidden place.
Streams whisper sweetly to the trees,
The soft serenade carried on the breeze.

Stars appear like notes in the night,
Filling the heavens with brilliant light.
In the artistry of the divine,
Creation sings, a love so fine.

Every heartbeat, a note of love,
A symphony played from the heavens above.
Together we join in this sacred song,
In the soft serenade, we all belong.

## The Unseen Hand of Compassion

In shadows deep, where sorrows dwell,
A gentle touch, we know so well.
The heart of grace, it seeks the lost,
To heal the wounds, despite the cost.

With whispered prayers that fill the air,
The unseen hand, it shows we care.
Through trials faced and burdens shared,
The light of love, forever bared.

In silent moments, breaths of peace,
From anguish's grip, we find release.
In every tear, a story flows,
Of hope renewed, where kindness grows.

So trust the path, though dark it seems,
For in the night, the spirit dreams.
An unseen grace, a guiding force,
The hand of compassion shows its course.

## Emissaries of the Divine

We are the threads in heaven's loom,
The light that breaks through shadows' gloom.
With hearts aflame, we walk the earth,
Proclaiming love, proclaiming worth.

In service, we find our true delight,
As emissaries of the holy light.
With every gesture, every word,
We spread the joy that must be heard.

In every soul, a spark divine,
A quiet glow, a sacred sign.
United, strong, we stand as one,
To chase away what must be shun.

With hands outstretched, we face the crowd,
In humble hearts, we were endowed.
For we are chosen, pure and free,
To echo love's eternity.

## Tapestry of Eternal Blessings

Threads of grace, intricately spun,
A tapestry woven, each soul has won.
In every stitch, a prayer is sewn,
In colors bright, our light has grown.

From joys and tears, the patterns rise,
Reflecting dreams that touch the skies.
Each moment shared, a sacred tie,
Binding us close as time passes by.

In union found, the heart expands,
A dance of faith, where fate commands.
As blessings flow from high above,
We find our strength in endless love.

So let us cherish every thread,
A miracle in love we've spread.
In life's design, we find our place,
A tapestry woven by endless grace.

**Songs of the Seraphim**

In realms of light, where angels sing,
The seraphim take flight on wing.
Their voices rise in perfect tune,
A melody beneath the moon.

With every note, the heavens sway,
They weave a magic, night and day.
In harmony, their souls align,
Echoes sweet, a love divine.

Through trials faced, their songs remain,
A guide for hearts in joy and pain.
With wings of fire, they soar above,
Reminders of eternal love.

So let us join this sacred choir,
And lift our voices ever higher.
In every heart, their message frames,
The songs of seraphim, love's flames.

# **The Soft Chorus of Faith**

In whispers of dawn, grace unfurls,
Hearts uplifted in quiet swirls.
Through trials faced, hope shines bright,
A soft chorus sings, guiding the light.

With each step taken, spirits soar,
Boundless love opens every door.
In the stillness, a promise rings,
Faith in harmony, as the heart sings.

As rivers flow, we find our way,
Together we stand, come what may.
In every shadow, the light will reign,
A soft chorus where joy remains.

When doubts arise, we seek the path,
In faith's embrace, we find our math.
A tapestry woven, strong and pure,
In the soft chorus, we find the cure.

## **Divine Echoes through the Veil**

Beyond the veil, the echoes sing,
Of love divine, our spirit's wing.
In the silence, a truth is shared,
In hearts that seek, His presence cared.

Through trials faced, grace abounds,
In whispered prayer, the heart resounds.
A melody soft, pure and near,
In the divine, we shed our fear.

In shadows deep, hope gently glows,
Through every tear, a river flows.
The echoes call, inviting us there,
To the arms of love, a sacred care.

In unity found, we rise anew,
With every step, the light breaks through.
Divine echoes, endless and bright,
Guide us ever towards the light.

## **Beneath Sacred Skies**

Beneath the skies, so vast and true,
In fields of grace, our spirits grew.
With every breath, the heavens sing,
In nature's arms, we find our spring.

Stars above, like dreams that shine,
In their glow, our hearts align.
Through storms and calm, a journey unfolds,
Beneath sacred skies, our faith holds.

With open hearts, we seek the light,
In every shadow, hope ignites.
Together we walk, hand in hand,
Beneath sacred skies, we understand.

In prayerful whispers, souls connect,
In every moment, we reflect.
Beneath the skies, in love we soar,
In faith's embrace, we seek for more.

## **Silent Testaments of the Heart**

In stillness found, our hearts obey,
Silent testaments lead the way.
Through trials faced, we learn to trust,
In every moment, love is a must.

With gentle grace, our spirits blend,
In sacred silence, we comprehend.
A language pure, beyond mere word,
In silent whispers, truth is heard.

As seasons change, and rivers flow,
Through every loss, through every glow.
The heart attunes to faith's embrace,
Silent testaments, our saving grace.

In loving bonds, we find our place,
A tapestry woven, a sacred space.
Through every beat, we recognize,
Silent testaments, the heart's true prize.

**Luminescent Threads of Mercy**

In shadows deep, a light appears,
Threads of mercy calm our fears.
Woven hearts, united strong,
In faith we rise, where we belong.

With gentle hands, He guides our way,
In trials faced, we learn to sway.
Each whisper soft, a sacred grace,
In love's embrace, we find our place.

Hope ignites, a radiant flame,
In every loss, we find His name.
Through valleys low, His spirit soars,
A tapestry rich, forever more.

Rest assured, we're never alone,
In the quiet, His truth is shown.
With luminescent threads so fine,
We are His, and He is mine.

## The Gentle Call of the Spirit

In the stillness, hear the sound,
The Spirit's voice, so profound.
With every breath, a sacred prayer,
Awakening love, beyond compare.

Gentle whispers fill the air,
Guiding hearts, with tender care.
In every moment, seek and find,
The call of grace, to heal mankind.

As morning breaks, the light will rise,
Illuminating hidden skies.
With open hearts, let peace unfold,
The gentle call, a tale retold.

Listen closely, let it lead,
To paths of joy and righteous deed.
In every tear, a blessing shared,
The Spirit's love, forever bared.

## **Serene Reflections of the Blessed**

In tranquil waters, wisdom flows,
Reflections bright of love that grows.
Each grateful thought, a star that shines,
In harmony, our heart entwines.

As twilight falls, we pause and pray,
In serendipity, we find our way.
With every moment, joy we trace,
In peaceful silence, we embrace.

The blessed path, where grace abounds,
In simple acts, true beauty found.
A melody of hearts in tune,
Echoes softly, morning's boon.

Together we walk, hand in hand,
A journey blessed, a sacred stand.
In every smile, a story's told,
Serene reflections, a heart of gold.

## **A Tapestry of Celestial Love**

Threads of starlight, woven dear,
In a tapestry that draws us near.
Each color bright, each pattern true,
Celestial love, forever new.

In every moment, hopes entwine,
The divine grace that feels like wine.
With every stitch, a prayer is said,
In unity, our spirits led.

As night unveils the heavens wide,
We find solace, in love we bide.
In gentle hues, the dawn will glow,
A gift of faith, our hearts will know.

Together we weave, through joy and strife,
A sacred bond, the pulse of life.
In every heart, His love remains,
A tapestry bright, where peace sustains.

## Heartbeats of the Divine within Us

In every pulse, a sacred hymn,
The breath of God, our hearts do brim.
With each heartbeat, grace flows near,
A whisper soft, a love sincere.

Through trials faced, we stand as one,
In darkest night, we seek the sun.
With faith our guide, we rise above,
United in this bond of love.

In silence deep, the truth we find,
Guided gently, hand in hand, we bind.
Our spirits soar, a dance divine,
The heartbeat echoes, we align.

Together woven, threads of light,
In God's embrace, we find our might.
As heartbeats merge, we sing our song,
In love's sweet arms, we all belong.

# Threads of Faith Interwoven with Love

A tapestry of hope we weave,
In every heart, a truth believes.
With threads of faith, we craft our fate,
In love entwined, we celebrate.

Through trials faced, we stand steadfast,
In unity, our bond is cast.
Each story shared, a sacred thread,
In every word, His promise spread.

With every tear, a seed we sow,
In darkened days, our spirits glow.
Together strong, we rise anew,
In faith and love, forever true.

A fabric rich, with colors bright,
In joy and pain, we seek the light.
Hand in hand, we walk the path,
With threads of faith, we share His wrath.

**Whispers Carried on Angel's Wings**

Softly spoken, words of grace,
In stillness found, a warm embrace.
With every breath, a prayer shall rise,
In whispers sweet, our spirits fly.

On wings of light, they come to aid,
In shadows deep, our fears they fade.
A gentle touch, a guiding hand,
In love's pure light, we understand.

From realms above, sweet voices call,
In every heart, they bear our all.
With angel's wings, we are set free,
In sacred love, our spirits see.

In tranquil night, their song we hear,
With faith and hope, we cast off fear.
Forever cherished, His love remains,
In every whisper, joy sustains.

## Seraphic Light in the Shadowed Vale

In valleys low, where shadows creep,
A seraph's light our souls shall keep.
Through darkest nights, we search for dawn,
With faith as guide, we carry on.

The softest glow breaks through the haze,
In every heart, a song of praise.
With courage strong, we face the plight,
In every tear, a spark of light.

And when despair seeks to confine,
The seraphic rays of love align.
In hope's embrace, our spirits soar,
Together strong, forevermore.

In shadowed vale, where tempests roar,
The light within shall ever soar.
With hearts aflame, we find our way,
In seraph's grace, we greet the day.

## **The Light of Forgiveness in the Darkness**

In shadows deep, where sorrows hide,
A whisper calls, a tranquil guide.
Forgiveness blooms, a radiant spark,
Illuminating paths once dark.

With every heart that learns to yield,
The burden lifts; the wounds are healed.
Grace flows freely, pure and bright,
As peace descends upon the night.

In tender moments, He imparts,
The balm of mercy to our hearts.
Transforming pain to love's embrace,
In darkness shines forgiveness' grace.

## An Altar of Stillness and Solitude

On quiet shores where silence reigns,
The soul retreats, the spirit gains.
A sacred space, where whispers dwell,
In solitude, we learn to tell.

The heart finds rest in gentle prayer,
With open arms and souls laid bare.
In stillness deep, the truth unfolds,
A sacred bond that never cold.

In every breath, a promise new,
A quiet altar, firm and true.
Where love abides and shadows cease,
In solitude, we find our peace.

## **Glistening Dewdrops of Blessed Promise**

At dawn's first light, the world awakes,
With dewdrops sweet, the earth remakes.
Each glistening bead, a gift divine,
Of hope renewed and love's design.

As petals bloom with morning's grace,
A fragrant breath in sacred space.
In nature's hands, our spirits swell,
With every drop, a tale to tell.

Beneath the sky, where dreams reside,
The promise shines; our hearts abide.
With faith adorned like morning dew,
Each drop reflects the love so true.

## The Dance of Grace in Life's Embrace


In every step, the rhythm flows,
A dance of grace, where loving glows.
Through joys and trials, hand in hand,
We twirl beneath the skies so grand.

With each heartbeat, a melody,
A sacred song, a hymn set free.
In laughter bright and tears that fall,
The dance of life unites us all.

Embracing shadows, light we find,
In every movement, hearts entwined.
Together, we will rise and weave,
The tapestry of love we leave.

**Echoes of Serenity in the Silence**

In the quiet dusk of day,
Whispers of peace softly sway.
Hearts align with gentle grace,
Finding joy in a sacred space.

In the stillness, souls unite,
Bathed in love, pure and bright.
Every breath, a prayer profound,
In silence, true solace is found.

A melody of soft sighs,
Underneath the endless skies.
Echoes rise, a hallowed song,
Guiding wayward souls along.

Beneath the stars, the spirit soars,
In the calm, the heart explores.
Embraced by warmth, we find our way,
In echoes of dawn's new day.

**Hymns of Hope in Wandering Shadows**

In the depths where shadows lie,
Hope emerges, a gentle sigh.
Whispers of light through the gloom,
Each note a promise to bloom.

With every step, the spirit sings,
Through darkened paths, the heart takes wings.
Faith ignites the night's embrace,
Filling voids with love's grace.

Hymns resound in the heart's retreat,
Guiding the lost, a sacred beat.
In wandering moments, the soul can find,
Strength in grace, and peace of mind.

Braving storms, we reach for skies,
In shadows where our spirit flies.
Trusting the dawn will bring the light,
We sing of hope, embracing the night.

## **The Sacred Language of Stillness**

In stillness lies the sacred word,
Whispered softly, yet often unheard.
The heart listens to what's profound,
In silence, true wisdom is found.

Each pause, a breath, a moment divine,
Time slows down in the quiet line.
A language formed in whispered prayers,
Binding souls in love's affairs.

In the hush, the spirit wakes,
Awake to truth, the heart partakes.
Vows of peace, a promise to keep,
In the language of stillness, we weep.

Embrace the calm, let worries cease,
In the silence, discover peace.
Within each heartbeat, hear the call,
The sacred language unites us all.

## **Glimmers of Faith in the Dark**

In the void where shadows creep,
Glimmers of faith begin to leap.
A flicker bright amidst despair,
A whisper carried in the air.

When night descends and hope feels far,
We search for truth, a guiding star.
With every tear, a promise breaks,
In the darkness, light awakes.

Each spark, a reminder to believe,
In stormy winds, we learn to cleave.
The heart ignites with courage anew,
Faith's glimmer leads us through.

From shadows deep, our spirits rise,
Embracing light beyond the skies.
In the dark, together we stand,
Glimmers of faith, a radiant band.

## **The Solace of Holy Presence**

In shadows deep, a light does gleam,
A gentle touch, like heaven's beam.
With every breath, a prayer we weave,
In holy grace, we dare believe.

The heart finds peace in whispered prayers,
In silence shared with sacred layers.
Though trials rise like stormy seas,
In faith, our souls find calm and ease.

The warmth of love, in presence felt,
In every tear, a truth is knelt.
A balm for wounds, both seen and bare,
In solace deep, we meet Him there.

Through all our days, He walks beside,
In joy and pain, our faithful guide.
Amidst the noise, His voice is clear,
In holy presence, we draw near.

## **Enveloped in Celestial Care**

Upon the dawn, His mercy shines,
In gentle hues, our spirits twine.
With every dawn, His love bestowed,
A tender hand upon the road.

In fields of grace, we wander free,
Embraced by love, we simply be.
The stars above, His promise bright,
In darkest hours, they give us light.

With every heartbeat, blessings flow,
In sacred trust, our hearts will grow.
Through valleys low and mountains high,
We sense His love, it's our reply.

In moments small, His truth prevails,
In whispered winds, we hear His tales.
Enveloped close, we sing His praise,
In every breath, our souls ablaze.

## Harmonics of Unseen Blessings

In quiet nights, the stars align,
A symphony of grace divine.
Each note, a gift, in silence shared,
Unseen blessings, tenderly bared.

With every trial, we grow anew,
In sacred bonds, our faith held true.
Each tear a tune, each joy a rhyme,
In harmony, we transcend time.

The whisper soft, the echo clear,
In sacred moments, we draw near.
Each heartbeat plays a part in song,
In dance of faith, we all belong.

In every pause, we hear the grace,
In unseen realms, we find our place.
Harmonics rise, our spirits soar,
In blessed cadence, forevermore.

## **A Symphony of Seraphic Whispers**

In twilight's hush, the angels sing,
A symphony of hope they bring.
With every note, a prayer ascends,
In woven light, our spirit mends.

The echoes warm, as hearts align,
In sacred space, the stars combine.
With every sigh, a promise made,
In seraph's breath, our fears do fade.

In vibrant hues, the heavens glow,
A tapestry of love to flow.
Through trials faced, we rise and sway,
In whispers sweet, we find our way.

So lift your voice, let praises ring,
In harmony, our hearts take wing.
A seraph's song, forever clear,
In symphony, we draw Him near.

# **Light Beyond the Horizon**

In shadows deep, a beacon glows,
A promise bright that gently shows.
Through trails of doubt, we seek our way,
With faith as guide, we'll find the day.

As dawn unfolds, the night takes flight,
Illumined paths in morning light.
With hearts attuned to whispered grace,
We walk in love, our rightful place.

Beneath the vast, resplendent skies,
Hope kindles dreams where silence lies.
The light we share, a sacred bond,
A journey shared, of which we're fond.

Beyond the veil, where visions near,
We rise on wings, devoid of fear.
Together bound, through endless time,
In unity, our souls will climb.

## Ethereal Murmurs of the Soul

In quietude, the spirit speaks,
A gentle breeze, a solace seeks.
The whispers soft, like morning dew,
Reveal the light that's born anew.

With every breath, a hymn of peace,
In shadows cast, the burdens cease.
Each tear a prayer, a heartfelt plea,
Connected by love, eternally free.

The echoes dance beneath the stars,
In sacred bonds, we're never far.
Each note of grace, a lullaby,
Embraced by realms where angels fly.

In realms unseen, our spirits soar,
To realms where grief can touch no more.
Together in this sacred space,
We find our home, our timeless place.

## **Celestial Embrace in the Night**

Beneath the quilt of velvet skies,
The moonlight bathes in soft replies.
Each star a spark of hope's embrace,
A guiding light, full of grace.

With every breath, we sync our hearts,
In whispered prayers, life's sacred arts.
The midnight air, a balm so sweet,
Where dreams and faith entwined will meet.

The night reveals the truths we seek,
In shadows deep, the silence speaks.
With open arms, we welcome light,
In ethereal dance, we take flight.

In every heart, a spark of flame,
A journey bright, yet never the same.
Together woven, in love's embrace,
Celestial paths lead us to grace.

## **Gracenotes on the Breeze**


In every leaf, a whisper sings,
A gentle touch of ancient wings.
The wind carries sweet melodies,
Through golden fields and whispering trees.

Each note a blessing, softly spoken,
In nature's choir, no heart is broken.
With every sigh, the earth responds,
A symphony of grace beyond.

In sunlit glades, the spirit sways,
With open hearts, we share our days.
The breezes dance, a sacred song,
In harmony, where we belong.

And when the night draws close its veil,
The gracenotes in the darkness trail.
With faith as ours, we ride the breeze,
In love's embrace, we're always free.

**Embraced by Heavenly Light**

In shadows deep, a beacon gleams,
A tender glow that softly beams.
With open arms, the spirit soars,
To heavenly heights, forevermore.

In every heart, His whisper glows,
A warmth that all creation knows.
We walk in grace, we trust the way,
In love's embrace, we choose to stay.

The stars align, a cosmic sign,
Pointing to love, both pure and divine.
Through trials faced, His light will shine,
A promise made, forever thine.

So let your soul, to Him, take flight,
Embraced always by heavenly light.

**The Subtle Song of Redemption**

In silence soft, the heart does hear,
A song of hope that draws us near.
It whispers gently through the night,
A melody of purest light.

Forgiveness flows like morning dew,
A balm for souls, a love so true.
With every note, a burden fades,
In grace's arms, our debt is laid.

The chorus sings of hearts reborn,
A tapestry of love, well-worn.
In every beat, the truth we find,
A subtle song that binds mankind.

So lift your voice, let praises rise,
In this sweet song, our spirits tie.

## **Echoes Across the Infinite**

In whispered tones, the cosmos speaks,
Its echoes dance as time seeks.
Each moment shared, a sacred thread,
Connecting hearts where love is spread.

From stars that shine to oceans' call,
In nature's grace, we find our all.
The universe in harmony,
Reflects the depth of purity.

Every sigh, a prayer that flies,
Across the vast and endless skies.
These echoes weave the stories told,
Of faith and love, of hearts bold.

So listen close, let silence guide,
In echoes deep, His truth confides.

## **Traces of Love in Every Breath**

In every breath, a hint of grace,
A gentle reminder of love's embrace.
We draw in hope with every sigh,
And feel the warmth as moments fly.

With open hearts, we seek the divine,
In life's sweet dance, our souls entwine.
A testament in each heartbeat,
Of mercy's power, bittersweet.

Through trials faced and bridges burned,
In every lesson, truth is learned.
In every tear, in every smile,
Love traces paths that stretch a mile.

So cherish each precious breath you take,
For in love's light, we shall awake.

## **Starlit Vows of Eternal Trust**

Under the vast and whispered skies,
We pledge our souls, where love complies.
Stars above, our witness true,
In sacred vows, we start anew.

Hearts entwined like vines of gold,
In faith we stand, both brave and bold.
Guided by light, we seek the way,
Eternal trust, come what may.

Through trials faced, our spirits rise,
In silence heard, the softest cries.
With every breath, a prayer we weave,
In starlit nights, we dare believe.

Together through the bends and turns,
A flame ignites, forever burns.
In celestial paths, our stories blend,
With each embrace, we ascend.

## **The Harmonies of Grace in Chaos**

Amidst the storms that swirl and rage,
A melody plays on wisdom's page.
With trembling hands, we raise our song,
In chaos, we find where we belong.

Each note a whisper of divine embrace,
In tangled roots, we find our space.
Harmony blooms in the fiercest night,
Guided by faith, we seek the light.

When shadows fall and fears arise,
We gather strength in each other's skies.
Surrendered hearts, we learn to trust,
In grace we stand, in hope we must.

The world may twist, but we shall sing,
In every trial, our spirits spring.
Together we rise, through thick and thin,
In chaos, the harmony begins.

# **Echoes of Intercession in the Quiet**

In the silence, prayers take flight,
Whispers of hope pierce through the night.
Each heartache shared, a sacred bond,
In quietude, we journey beyond.

Through gentle sighs and longing calls,
We seek the solace when darkness falls.
Interceding souls, united we stand,
Holding each other, hand in hand.

In stillness, our spirits rise above,
A tapestry woven with threads of love.
Each echo heard transcends all fears,
A chorus formed from our deepest tears.

The sacred space where silence reigns,
Is where we heal from our hidden pains.
With open hearts, we share the weight,
In quiet grace, we cultivate fate.

## **The Subtle Dance of Destiny's Hand**

With every step, our paths align,
In the dance of fate, a love divine.
Held in the arms of time's soft sway,
We move to rhythms that guide our way.

The subtle whispers of dreams unspoken,
In destiny's waltz, hearts unbroken.
Each turn, each spin, a tale retold,
In the embrace of threads of gold.

In fleeting moments, we find our place,
The beauty of time, a gentle grace.
In shadows cast, our laughter gleams,
Choreographed steps inspire our dreams.

As stars align, we trust the plan,
In divine motion, hand in hand.
Together we weave our sacred strand,
In the subtle dance of destiny's hand.

# **Echoes of Celestial Light**

In the stillness, whispers rise,
Guided by the stars in the skies.
The heart beats in divine refrain,
Echoing love that knows no pain.

Each dawn brings a promise bright,
Awakening souls to sacred light.
From the depths of twilight's fall,
We find our strength in the celestial call.

The moon sings soft, a lullaby,
Cradling dreams that soar and fly.
In shadows cast by faith's embrace,
We seek the warmth of timeless grace.

Together we walk, hand in hand,
United by a love so grand.
With each step, our spirits rise,
To meet the echoes in the skies.

## **Threads of Holy Kindness**

In moments shared, we weave our fate,
With threads of kindness, we create.
Each gesture, a spark of light,
Binding hearts in the silence of night.

Through trials faced, compassion grows,
In every struggle, kindness flows.
A gentle touch, a soft-spoken word,
Can heal the wounds that once occurred.

In laughter shared, we find our peace,
As love's sweet symphony may never cease.
In the tapestry of life we find,
The sacred bond of heart and mind.

Together we stand, side by side,
Guided by grace, in love we abide.
Threads of holy kindness, intertwined,
In the fabric of our souls, divinely designed.

## **Beneath the Veil of Mercy**

Beneath the veil, where shadows dwell,
Lies a sanctuary, a sacred well.
In the quiet, we seek the truth,
Wrapped in mercy, embracing our youth.

The tears we shed, like rain from the skies,
Nourish the earth, and help us rise.
In the gentle arms of love we find,
A healing balm for the weary mind.

With every prayer, the soul ascends,
A bridge of hope where sorrow ends.
Together in faith, we lift our gaze,
Finding strength in the radiant rays.

Through trials faced, and storms withstood,
Mercy's light transforms our good.
Beneath the veil, we come alive,
In the heart of grace, forever we thrive.

## **The Embrace of Sacred Silence**

In the hush of night, a stillness reigns,
Washing away our worldly pains.
In sacred silence, we can hear,
The quiet call that draws us near.

The weight of chaos fades away,
As whispers guide us in gentle sway.
In moments lost, we find the whole,
The embrace of peace that fills the soul.

With every breath, we learn to trust,
In silence deep, our spirits adjust.
Among the stars, where echoes play,
We seek the light that shows the way.

Together, we walk this sacred path,
In the warmth of love's gentle bath.
In the embrace of quiet grace,
We find our home, our resting place.

Milton Keynes UK
Ingram Content Group UK Ltd.
UKHW020903041224
451843UK00022B/126